A Special Gift

For: Grammy

From: Raye

Date: Sat May 12, 2001

Illustration Copyright ©1999 Judy Buswell
Text Copyright ©1999

The Brownlow Corporation
6309 Airport Freeway
Fort Worth, Texas 76117

Grateful appreciation is expressed to
Lara Lleverino for her research assistance.

ISBN: 1-57051-196-9
Printed by Palace Press Hong Kong

Grandmother

Compiled and Written by Caroline Brownlow

Illustrated by *Judy Buswell*

Brownlow

Little Treasures Miniature Books

There's no place
like home—
except Grandma's!

ANONYMOUS

Give God the blossom of the
day. Do not put Him off
with faded leaves.

ANONYMOUS

❧❦❧

The future belongs to those
who believe in the beauty
of their dreams.

ELEANOR ROOSEVELT

Full maturity is achieved by realizing
that you have choices to make.

ANGELA BARRON MCBRIDE

❧

Parents have lots of trouble solving
their children's problems, and
children have even more trouble
solving their parents' problems.

ANONYMOUS

I Never Knew

I never understood just how much love my grandparents felt for me while they were alive. Yes, I knew they liked me and loved me. But I had no way of knowing the depth and extent of their love until I had a grandson myself. He doesn't have *to do* anything! I delight in his mere presence. He will never really know the full measure of my love while I am alive, but hopefully someday he will understand.

P.C.B.

Though we travel the world over
to find the beautiful, we must
carry it with us, or we find it not.

R.W.E.

May the Lord bless you all the
days of your life, and may you live
to see your children's children.

Psalm 128:5, 6

He's Doing Better

A little girl was sitting in her grandmother's lap one day. Grandmother was old and her face was very wrinkled. Suddenly, the girl asked, "Grandma, did God make you?" The grandmother lovingly replied, "Yes, honey, He did." The girl then asked, "And did God make me?" Grandma answered again, "Yes, honey, He did." After a moment the little girl concluded, "Grandma, don't you think God is doing a better job now than He used to?"

It is the sweet simple
things of life which are
the real ones after all.

LAURA INGALLS WILDER

❧

From the lips of children
and infants you have
ordained praise.

PSALM 8:2

No cowboy was ever faster on the draw than a grandparent pulling a baby picture out of a wallet.

ANONYMOUS

⊱⟐⊰

Cheerfulness and content are great beautifiers and are famous preservers of youthful looks.

CHARLES DICKENS

If becoming a grandmother
was only a matter of choice,
I would advise every one of you
straight away to become one.
There is no fun for older
people like it.

HANNAH WHITALL SMITH

I love little children,
and it is not a slight thing
when they, who are so
fresh from God, love us.

CHARLES DICKENS

⚬⚭⚬

A grandmother's patience
is like a tube of toothpaste—
it's never quite all gone.

I Loved It

Surely now in my latter years I'll be able to put to good use what wisdom I have accumulated. Instead, I have been going through one of the most intense learning periods of my life. Especially in connection with our children and grandchildren.

I loved being a grandmother. Not since I was a small girl had I had so much fun. Not only that, I learned volumes about the delight of living in the Kingdom of God while still on this earth.

CATHERINE MARSHALL

If only we'd stop trying to
be happy, we could have a
pretty good time.

EDITH WHARTON

❧❧❧

Everyone needs beauty. . . places
to play in and pray in where nature
may heal and cheer and give
strength to the body and soul alike.

JOHN MUIR

Some lives, like evening
primroses, blossom most
beautifully in the evening of life.

CHARLES E. COWMAN

⥱⥬⥱

The grandmother of today
has something that the
grandmother of the past didn't
have—blond hair.

ANONYMOUS

A sweater is a knitted garment
worn by a child when
his grandmother feels cold.

ANONYMOUS

❦

Children's children are a crown
to the aged, and parents are the
pride of their children.

PROVERBS 17:6

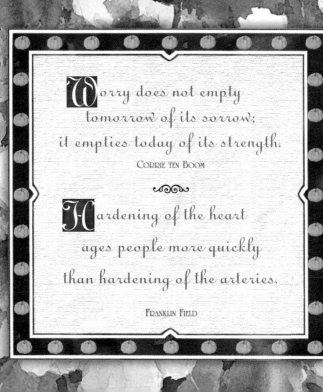

Worry does not empty
tomorrow of its sorrow;
it empties today of its strength.

CORRIE TEN BOOM

❧⳾⳾❧

Hardening of the heart
ages people more quickly
than hardening of the arteries.

FRANKLIN FIELD

Becoming
Important to a Child

A hundred years from now it will not matter what my bank account was, the sort of house I lived in, or the kind of car I drove. But the world may be different because I was important in the life of a child.

A Child and a Candy Bar

One good thing about inflation is that it's practically impossible now for a youngster to get sick on a five-cent candy bar.

ANONYMOUS

Ordinary Things

God does not want us to do extraordinary things; He wants us to do the ordinary things extraordinarily well.

To show a child what once
delighted you, to find the child's
delight added to your own—
this is happiness.

J.B.P.

∽✤∾

In youth we learn;
in age we understand.

MARIE VON EBNER-ESCHENBACH

Growing up means choosing
to meet someone else's need
rather than your own.

⁂

If you think spanking
is not necessary the chances are
you're a grandparent.

The Lord has done
great things for us and
we are filled with joy.

PSALM 126:3

⊱⊰

Children are messengers
we send to a time
we will not see.

We are always
the same age inside.

GERTRUDE STEIN

❖❖❖

Many a child is spoiled
because you can't spank
his grandmother.

ANONYMOUS

Youth is not
a time of life.
It is a state
of mind.